AF228530

BABY GOATS

by Martha London

Cody Koala

An Imprint of Pop!
popbooksonline.com

abdobooks.com

Published by Pop!, a division of ABDO, PO Box 398166, Minneapolis, Minnesota 55439. Copyright © 2021 by POP, LLC. International copyrights reserved in all countries. No part of this book may be reproduced in any form without written permission from the publisher. Pop!™ is a trademark and logo of POP, LLC.

Printed in the United States of America, North Mankato, Minnesota

052020
092020

THIS BOOK CONTAINS RECYCLED MATERIALS

Cover Photo: G. Lacz/Arco Images GmbH/Alamy
Interior Photos: G. Lacz/Arco Images GmbH/Alamy, 1; Shutterstock Images, 5 (top), 5 (bottom left), 5 (bottom right), 6–7, 9, 10, 13 (top), 13 (bottom left), 13 (bottom right), 14, 17, 19, 20–21

Editor: Nick Rebman
Series Designer: Christine Ha

Library of Congress Control Number: 2019955132
Publisher's Cataloging-in-Publication Data
Names: London, Martha, author.
Title: Baby goats / by Martha London
Description: Minneapolis, Minnesota : POP!, 2021 | Series: Baby farm animals | Includes online resources and index
Identifiers: ISBN 9781532167447 (lib. bdg.) | ISBN 9781532168543 (ebook)
Subjects: LCSH: Goats--Infancy--Juvenile literature. | Kids (Goats)--Juvenile literature. | Baby farm animals--Juvenile literature. | Animal babies--Juvenile literature.
Classification: DDC 636.3/9--dc23

Hello! My name is

Cody Koala

Pop open this book and you'll find QR codes like this one, loaded with information, so you can learn even more!

Scan this code* and others like it while you read, or visit the website below to make this book pop.

popbooksonline.com/baby-goats

*Scanning QR codes requires a web-enabled smart device with a QR code reader app and a camera.

Table of Contents

Just a Kid

Baby goats are called kids. Kids are **mammals**. They are born with short, soft fur. Kids are born in a barn. The barn has straw on the floor.

Watch a video here!

A baby goat can stand soon after birth. One of the first things the baby goat does is eat. It drinks its mother's milk.

Run, Jump, and Climb

Mother goats watch their kids. Kids are **social**. They spend time with other young goats. Kids play with one another. They run and kick.

Complete an
activity here!

ear
tail
eye
leg
hoof

Goats have hard **hooves**. Their hooves are split into two parts. For this reason, goats are excellent climbers. Kids begin to climb and jump off tree stumps when they are one week old.

One kind of goat climbs trees to eat fruit.

Chapter 3

Growing Up

Baby goats drink their mother's milk. Milk has important **nutrients** in it. The milk helps kids grow strong. As kids get older, they try new foods.

Learn more here!

Baby goats have to get used to solid food. Farmers give kids small amounts of hay when they are one week old.

Kids stop drinking milk when they are three months old. At this time, they can eat solid food all the time. Goats eat hay. They also eat vegetables and fruit.

Chapter 4

Fully Grown Goats

Farmers raise goats for many reasons. Some raise goats for meat and milk. Others raise goats with long hair. Farmers sell the hair to people who make yarn.

Learn more here!

Some people keep goats as pets. Goats can be friendly. But goats need to stay in a **herd**. Goats may break things if they are lonely.

Making Connections

Text-to-Self

Imagine you are on a farm. What would it be like to see a baby goat?

Text-to-Text

What other books about baby animals have you read? How are baby goats similar to and different from those animals?

Text-to-World

Some farmers raise goats for milk. What other kinds of milk do people drink?

Glossary

herd – a large group of animals that live and travel together.

hooves – the hard parts that cover an animal's feet.

mammal – a type of animal that has hair or fur and feeds milk to its young.

nutrient – part of food that humans, animals, and plants need to stay strong and healthy.

social – enjoying the company of others.

Index

Online Resources

popbooksonline.com

Thanks for reading this Cody Koala book!

Scan this code* and others like it in this book, or visit the website below to make this book pop!

popbooksonline.com/baby-goats

*Scanning QR codes requires a web-enabled smart device with a QR code reader app and a camera.